CÁDIZ
TRAVEL GUIDE 2024

Discover Cádiz's hidden gems and ancient wonders in 2024 edition

Jay Pittman

COPYRIGHT © 2023 BY JAY PITTMAN

Reserved rights apply. Without the publisher's prior written consent, no portion of this publication may be copied, distributed, or transmitted in any way, including by photocopying, recording, or other mechanical or electronic means, with the exception of brief quotations used in critical reviews and other noncommercial uses allowed by copyright law.

TABLE OF CONTENTS

CHAPTER ONE: INTRODUCTION

CHAPTER TWO: GETTING THERE

CHAPTER THREE: ACCOMMODATIONS

CHAPTER FOUR: EXPLORING THE CITY

CHAPTER FIVE: CULTURAL EXPERIENCES

CHAPTER SIX: CUISINE OF CÁDIZ

CHAPTER SEVEN: DAY TRIPS AND EXCURSIONS

CHAPTER EIGHT: OUTDOOR ACTIVITIES

CHAPTER NINE: NIGHTLIFE

CHAPTER TEN: SHOPPING

CHAPTER ELEVEN: PRACTICAL INFORMATION

CHAPTER TWELVE: CONCLUSION

CHAPTER ONE: INTRODUCTION

Welcome to Cádiz

Welcome to Cádiz, a historic and culturally rich city tucked away on Spain's southwest coast. As you go through this enchanted location, you'll find that the vitality of current life is interlaced with an antique charm. Due to its distinctive geographic form, Cadiz is often referred to as the "Silver Teacup" and is a treasure trove of experiences just waiting to be discovered.

Brief History of Cádiz

With origins dating back thousands of years, Cadiz is among the oldest continually inhabited towns in Europe. Established about 1104 BC by the Phoenicians, this port played a crucial role in facilitating commerce between different cultures. It saw the rise and fall of many empires throughout the ages, including the Moors, Romans, Visigoths, and Carthaginians.

During the Age of Exploration, the city's strategic significance increased to a new level as it served as a departure point for expeditions to the New World. The architecture, food, and customs of Cádiz provide witness to the irreversible impact that the period's inflow of money and cross-cultural interaction had on the city.

Additionally, Cádiz had a big impact on Spanish history, especially during the Spanish Civil War and the Napoleonic Wars. Its fortitude carried it through difficult times, and now tourists may explore the ruins of these past eras in the city's museums, forts, and winding lanes.

Wander through the Old Town's winding lanes, and you'll come across architectural treasures like the Cathedral of Cádiz, a masterwork that masterfully combines Baroque and Neoclassical styles. Squares around the city, including Plaza de España, act as social centers where visitors and residents congregate to take in the vibrant atmosphere.

What's New in the 2024 Edition

Travelers may look forward to some new additions in the 2024 edition of Cádiz Exploration. The waterfront promenade's renovation is one of its most notable characteristics. This region, which was once a hidden treasure, is now known for its hip cafés, art installations, and expansive vistas of the Atlantic Ocean. It is evidence of Cádiz's dedication to blending its old-world elegance with modern conveniences.

Furthermore, 2024 sees a growing emphasis on eco-friendly travel. Cádiz has put in place eco-friendly measures such as zones designated for pedestrians, bicycle sharing programs, and conservation efforts to protect the surrounding environment. In order to preserve the natural beauty of the area for future generations, the city strives to strike a balance between the flood of tourists and its environmental preservation efforts.

In the 2024 edition, Cadiz has embraced technology, launching cutting-edge guided tours via augmented reality applications. With interactive features that bring the past to life, these digital companions provide immersive experiences while recounting the history of the city. Discovering historic landmarks and ancient ruins from a contemporary perspective helps visitors better appreciate Cádiz's enthralling story.

Foodies will like the new gastronomic offerings that will be available in 2024. The culinary culture of Cadiz has developed, bringing in delicacies from throughout the world while maintaining its local characteristics. Modern fusion eateries and century-old tapas bars coexist, providing a wide variety of choices to suit any taste.

Additionally, the 2024 edition shows an increased emphasis on cultural festivals and activities. Cádiz has organized an annual calendar that includes traditional flamenco performances, art exhibits, and music festivals to honor its rich cultural past. This guarantees that guests, whatever the season, may fully engage with the local way of life.

Finally, Cádiz welcomes you to explore its timeless streets and experience the tasteful fusion of the past and present.

CHAPTER TWO: GETTING THERE

Southwest Spain's Cádiz is a charming old city with a wealth of culture, history, and breathtaking scenery. A seamless and pleasurable trip depends on your ability to navigate the city and comprehend your alternatives for getting around, whether you're here for business or a relaxing vacation. We will examine the several modes of transportation in Cadiz in this extensive guide, along with helpful arrival advice to make the most of your trip.

Transportation Options

1. Air Travel: Jerez Airport (XRY), which is around 44 kilometers away, is the nearest major airport to Cadiz since it does not have its own airport. Seville Airport (SVQ), which is around 125 kilometers from Cádiz, is an additional feasible option. Flights to important cities in Spain and Europe are available from both airports, linking Cadiz with other destinations worldwide.

2. Train Services: Cadiz has a well-established, effective rail system. Travelers will find Estación de Cádiz, the city's principal rail station, conveniently placed in the center of town. Regular services are provided by the national railway operator, Renfe, between Cadiz and important towns like Seville, Madrid, and Barcelona. A nice addition to your trip is the picturesque train ride along the coastline.

3. Bus Networks: Cádiz is well served by a vast bus network, which offers an economical and adaptable form of transportation. While intercity buses connect Cádiz to neighboring towns and cities, local buses connect the city's many neighborhoods. Two significant bus companies that operate in the area and provide both short- and long-distance services are ALSA and Comes.

4. Ferry Services: Cadiz may be reached by ferry due to its coastal position. El Puerto de Santa María and Rota, two neighboring ports, are connected to Cadiz via ferry. The picturesque boat trip offers a distinctive viewpoint of the city and its environs. Ferry connections to the adjacent Canary Islands are also available.

5. Car Rentals: Hiring a car is a common choice for those who value independence and flexibility. In Cadiz, there are several car-rental companies that provide a variety of automobiles to accommodate various tastes. Travelers may explore the stunning surroundings and seaside roads at their own leisure while they drive through the city.

Arrival Tips
After discussing your alternatives for getting around, let's look at some helpful arrival advice to make your trip to Cádiz hassle-free and pleasant.

1. Currency and Banking: Make sure you have enough euros, the local currency, on hand to cover your early outlays. With so many of them scattered over the city, ATMs provide a handy option to take out cash. Although major credit cards are accepted almost everywhere, it's best to have cash for local businesses and marketplaces.

2. Language: Although English is widely spoken in tourist areas, Spanish is the official language. Acquiring a few fundamental Spanish words may improve your communication and show consideration for other cultures. Any attempt to speak in their language is much appreciated by the locals.

3. Lodging: Reserve your lodging well in advance, particularly during the busiest travel times. There are several alternatives available in Cadiz, ranging from beachside resorts to boutique hotels in the old city. When choosing your stay, take into account your tastes and the distance to popular sites.

4. Local Cuisine: Get acquainted with the food culture of the area. The seafood, tapas, and traditional Andalusian specialties of Cadiz are well-known. Discover local markets to enjoy fresh products and regional delicacies, including Cádiz's Central Market.

5. Public Transportation Cards: You should think about getting a transportation card if you want to use public transit often. These cards are a cheap way to see the city and its environs since they often provide reduced bus and rail costs.

6. Weather and Clothes: Cadiz has warm winters and scorching summers due to its Mediterranean environment. Be sure to pack appropriately for the season of your trip. It's a good idea to pack a hat, sunscreen, and comfortable walking shoes, particularly if you want to explore the city on foot.

7. Cultural Etiquette: Show consideration for regional traditions and conventions. Spanish people value manners; therefore, saying "gracias" (thank you) is courteous conduct. It's typical to tip servers in restaurants, generally by rounding up the amount.

8. Safety Measures: Most people agree that traveling to Cadiz is safe. But it's essential to maintain awareness, particularly in populated regions. In popular tourist areas, watch out for pickpockets and be mindful of your possessions.

In summary:
Worldwide, tourists are drawn to Cadiz by its breathtaking scenery, lively culture, and rich history. With a variety of transit choices, getting around the city is easy, and you can enjoy all of its

features. You may improve your trip and make treasured experiences in this alluring Spanish jewel by using the arrival advice given. Cádiz provides a tapestry of experiences just waiting to be explored, whether you prefer to stroll through its historic streets, indulge in regional cuisine, or unwind on its golden beaches.

CHAPTER THREE: ACCOMMODATIONS

In southwest Spain, the ancient port city of Cadiz has a variety of lodging options for those looking for style, comfort, and a one-of-a-kind experience. Travelers visiting Cádiz may choose from a wide range of accommodations to fit their tastes, including opulent hotels, quaint guesthouses, and really unusual stays.

Hotels

1. Cadiz Park
Situated on the Atlantic Ocean, the Parador de Cádiz is an opulent hotel that blends contemporary architecture with stunning vistas. With its modern architecture, roomy accommodations, and rooftop pool, it's no wonder that many choose it when looking for a high-end experience. While the hotel's

spa promotes rest and renewal, its restaurant serves delicious Andalusian cuisine.

2. Accommodations La Catedral
The famous cathedral of Cádiz is close to Hotel La Catedral, which is tucked away in the center of the ancient town. Elegant rooms at this boutique hotel combine modern and traditional design elements, and there's a rooftop terrace with expansive views of the city and the sea for guests to enjoy. Easy access to local eateries, stores, and historical attractions is made possible by the location.

3. Hotel Playa Victoria
When looking for a beachside experience, the Playa Victoria Hotel is a great choice. This contemporary hotel provides spacious accommodations with views of the sea and overlooks La Victoria Beach. The hotel has direct access to the beach, a spa, and a number of eating choices. It's the perfect option for

anyone who wants to enjoy both beach relaxation and city discovery.

Guesthouses

1. The Caracol Casa

A little guesthouse in the center of the old town called Casa Caracol would be the ideal option if you'd rather stay in a more private area. This is a family-run business with a warm, welcoming vibe and beautifully furnished rooms that showcase the local way of life. A courtyard garden and the hosts' individual attention are available to guests.

2. Fantoni Hostel

Hostal Fantoni, which is close to the central market, provides inexpensive lodging without sacrificing comfort. The guesthouse offers basic yet cozy rooms as well as a shared kitchen for visitors. Because of its central position, exploring Cádiz's bustling streets, marketplaces, and historical sites is simple.

3. Palacio Casa Cádiz

The renovated 18th-century palace that serves as Casa Palacio Cádiz offers a distinctive guesthouse experience. The tastefully furnished apartments provide a window into the rich history of the city, showcasing a fusion of traditional and contemporary features. The center courtyard is charming and offers a peaceful area to unwind.

Unique Stays

1. Glamping Airstream in Cadiz

Consider Airstream Glamping Cádiz, where visitors may stay in vintage Airstream trailers, for a unique experience. This unusual lodging choice, which is situated in a tranquil area, combines comfort and excitement. Every trailer has contemporary conveniences, and the outside area lets visitors take in the scenery.

2. Accommodations in Lighthouses at Trafalgar Lighthouse

Consider spending your time at a lighthouse with a view of the Gibraltar Strait. That is just what the Lighthouse Accommodation at Faro de Trafalgar offers. Enjoy the beauty of a historic lighthouse and take in expansive views of the surrounding landscapes during your one-of-a-kind vacation. It's a very unique opportunity to engage with the marine heritage of the area.

3. La Playa Casa

Casa de la Playa provides a variety of distinctive lodging options, such as beach huts and bohemian-style cottages, for a beachside getaway with a twist. Guests may enjoy contemporary amenities while immersing themselves in nature at this eco-friendly hideaway. For those looking for something different from a typical vacation, the relaxed environment and close proximity to the beach provide a peaceful retreat.

To sum up, Cádiz offers a variety of lodging options to suit a range of interests and tastes. Every kind of tourist may find something to enjoy in Cádiz, whether they are looking for the lavishness of a five-star hotel, the warmth of a guesthouse, or the distinctiveness of alternative lodgings. The city is a popular travel destination because of its fascinating history, breathtaking architecture, and lively culture. Additionally, the wide range of lodging options guarantees that guests can find the ideal place to stay while traveling.

CHAPTER FOUR: EXPLORING THE CITY

Travelers are drawn to the historic city of Cadiz, which is tucked away on Spain's southwest coast and is known for its lively culture, rich history, and stunning scenery. Your tour guide will take you on an immersive tour of the city, where you will discover the captivating features of the Old Town, discover the cutting-edge attractions that embody Cádiz's modern vibe, and meander along the charming waterfront promenade that links the city to its maritime heritage.

Old Town Highlights

Antique Tapestry
The Old Town of Cadiz, which dates back more than 3,000 years, is a living reminder of the city's long past. Start your tour with the impressive

Puerta de Tierra, which serves as the entrance to the Old Town. The entrance to a maze-like system of winding cobblestone lanes and ancient squares is marked by this imposing arch.

Cádiz Cathedral

The magnificent Cathedral of Cadiz, which combines Baroque and Neoclassical architectural elements, is located in the center of Old Town. Enter and be amazed by the elaborate altars, elaborate chapels, and expansive views from the cathedral's towers that show off the layout of the city.

Tavira Torre

Climb the city's highest tower, the Torre Tavira, for a unique view of Cadiz. It was a watchtower at one point, but now it projects live views of Cadiz onto a concave surface, acting as a camera obscura. A mesmerizing vista of the Old Town, the Atlantic

Ocean, and the far-off shoreline may be seen from the 360-degree perspective.

The Flores Plaza

Explore the quaint Plaza de las Flores, a lively area with street performers, busy cafés, and colorful flower shops. It's the perfect place to take in the authentic vibe and have tapas while taking in the classic architecture of the Old Town.

The San Felipe Neri Oratorio

Learn the history of the Oratorio de San Felipe Neri, a prominent location where the first Spanish constitution was written in 1812. The structure is a must-see for history buffs because of its modest façade, which betrays the historical significance inside.

Beach La Caleta

Nestled between two medieval castles, La Caleta Beach is a great place to get away from the small streets and enjoy some sea air. With its golden beaches, placid waves, and views of Castillo de San Sebastián and Castillo de Santa Catalina, this urban beach provides a tranquil haven.

Modern Attractions

Cadiz Museum
Archaeology, anthropology, and art are all represented in the Cádiz Museum's collection, which spans from modern culture to history. Learn about the history of the city via artifacts and get a glimpse of the rich cultural fabric that makes up contemporary Cádiz.

Falla Grand Theater
Experience the arts at the Gran Teatro Falla, an architectural marvel that presents everything from flamenco acts to classical music. Rich acoustics and the theater's elaborate design make for a memorable cultural experience.

University of Cádiz

Discover the campus of Cádiz University, which combines contemporary and traditional architecture. The university's lively atmosphere and beachfront setting combine to provide a distinctive academic setting.

The Contemporary Art Space (ECCO)

ECCO offers a venue for cutting-edge exhibits and cultural activities for fans of modern art. By presenting the work of regional and worldwide artists who are pushing the limits of creative expression, this vibrant venue promotes innovation.

Market Central (Mercado Central)

Discover the tastes of Cadiz at the Mercado Central, a thriving open-air market where residents and tourists alike congregate to peruse booths filled with fresh vegetables, seafood, and local specialties. Interact with merchants, consume regional specialties, and take in the region's many gastronomic offerings.

Waterfront Promenade

The Marítimo Path
Wander the picturesque Paseo Marítimo, a waterfront boulevard that perfectly captures the spirit of Cádiz's maritime culture. This promenade, which is surrounded by palm trees and faces the Atlantic, offers a peaceful haven with expansive views of the city and the ocean.

The Victoria Beach
Continue your waterfront adventure at Cádiz's biggest and busiest beach, Playa de la Victoria. Soak in the sun, cool down with a swim, or enjoy water sports against the background of the city.

Park Genovés

Parque Genovés, a verdant botanical park next to the seafront, offers a peaceful haven. The park's winding trails, unique plants, and decorative fountains provide a tranquil haven for people to relax in the splendor of the natural world.

San Sebastián Castle
A causeway connects the fortified island of Castillo de San Sebastián to the city, marking the end of your waterfront stroll. The captivating sight created by the castle's silhouette against the setting sun represents Cádiz's unbreakable bond with the sea.

In summary
With a waterfront promenade that embraces the city's marine character, a contemporary attraction vibrating with cultural vitality, and an Old Town steeped in history, Cadiz beckons visitors on an enthralling trip. Whether exploring the city's historic neighborhoods, taking in cutting-edge artwork, or just enjoying the sea wind while

strolling down the promenade, Cadiz reveals itself as a complex location where the past and present live together. Discovering every aspect of this captivating city will surely lead you to realize how timeless its charm is, making Cádiz a treasure on Spain's southwest coast.

CHAPTER FIVE: CULTURAL EXPERIENCES

A city rich in culture and history, Cadiz enthralls both residents and tourists with its diverse array of cultural activities. Cádiz welcomes you to go on a trip through time and celebration with its array of museums and galleries, as well as its lively local festivals and events.

Museums and Galleries

1. Museum of Cadiz: Overview: With items tracing the history of the city from Phoenician antiquity to the present, the Museum of Cadiz is a cultural icon. Its holdings of fine art and archaeology reflect the wide range of influences that have formed Cadiz throughout the ages.
Highlights: A notable collection of Baroque paintings, Roman sculptures, and Phoenician

sarcophagi await visitors. In order to highlight Cadiz's significance as a vital port, the museum also showcases items from the city's nautical past.

2. Cádiz Cathedral Museum: Overview: Housed within the recognizable Cádiz Cathedral, this museum provides an insight into the local artistic and religious traditions. The cathedral itself is a magnificent example of Spanish Baroque architecture, and the museum deepens the visitor's comprehension of the building's history and purpose.

Highlights: Religious art, including paintings, sculptures, and liturgical artifacts, is on display in the museum. Discover the historical individuals' graves in the cathedral's crypt, then climb the tower for sweeping views of the city and the Atlantic Ocean.

3. Centro Cultural Reina Sofía: Overview: Housed in a former hospital, this cultural institution has developed into Cádiz's center for modern art. By organizing recurring concerts, seminars, and exhibits, it enhances the current cultural landscape of the city.

Highlights: Through provocative exhibits, visitors may interact with current Spanish and international artists. The center's dedication to promoting creativity is seen in its educational initiatives and activities that link local artists with the community.

4. Cádiz Carnival Museum: Overview: Cádiz's carnival is well known around the globe for its humor and enthusiasm. The Carnival Museum offers information on the origins and customs of this vibrant occasion, honoring the inventiveness and good humor that characterize Cádiz's carnival vibe.

Highlights: The museum allows visitors to feel the lively atmosphere all year long by displaying the costumes, masks, and musical instruments used in the Carnival. The distinctive spirit of the carnival is brought to life via interactive displays and multimedia shows.

Local Festivals and Events

1. Cádiz Carnival: Overview: A two-week spectacle of song, dancing, and satire, the Cádiz Carnival has been designated as a Festival of International Tourist Interest. People dress up in extravagant costumes and perform on the street, bringing pleasure and social criticism to the scene.

Highlights: Parades include intricate floats and vibrant costumes, while street chirigotas (musical ensembles) amuse audiences with clever tunes. The Carnival draws people from all over the globe because of its irreverent attitude and cultural importance, which make it a must-attend event.

2. Semana Santa (Holy Week): Overview: In Cádiz, Semana Santa is a well-observed religious and cultural occasion. Drums and somber music fill the air as intricate floats portraying various episodes from the Passion of Christ move through the city's streets in processions.

Highlights: Taking in the elaborate processions, in which religious brotherhoods lug bulky floats adorned with saint statues, is an enlightening cultural experience. The community spirit and reverence in the air are a reflection of Cádiz's enduring religious traditions.

3. Fiesta de la Virgen del Carmen: Synopsis: Cadiz is a seaside city with strong ties to the ocean. Celebrated with religious services, exuberant celebrations along the waterfront, and marine processions, the Fiesta de la Virgen del Carmen honors the patron saint of fishermen.

Highlights: The city's nautical history is showcased by the spectacle of the Virgen del Carmen statue being carried through the streets and onto boats for a maritime procession. Traditional dances, music, and fireworks all contribute to the joyous mood.

4. Cádiz Flamenco Festival: Overview: Held yearly in Cádiz, the Flamenco Festival honors flamenco, a passionate and expressive art form. Renowned flamenco performers from across the world come together for this event to provide riveting performances that highlight the city's strong links to this emotive musical style.

Highlights: During the festival's performances, fans of flamenco may immerse themselves in the creativity of dancers, guitarists, and vocalists. Visitors may also learn more about the origins of flamenco in Cádiz culture and its development via workshops and seminars.

In summary, Cadiz is a cultural treasure on the Andalusian coast, providing a wide variety of experiences that are a reflection of its dynamic past and rich present. Travelers visiting Cadiz are certain to experience a cultural tapestry that is both dynamic and intriguing, whether they want to explore museums that reveal the history of the city or take part in vibrant festivals that capture its essence.

CHAPTER SIX: CUISINE OF CÁDIZ

The charming coastal city of Cadiz, located in southwest Spain, has a gastronomic legacy that is strongly influenced by its many cultural influences and marine past. This piece dives into the rich culinary culture of Cádiz, highlighting must-try foods and well-liked eateries that epitomize the gastronomic experience in this captivating city.

Historical Influences: Thanks to centuries of maritime commerce and cross-cultural interactions, Cadiz's cuisine is a fascinating fusion of Moorish, Phoenician, and Andalusian influences. The city's closeness to the Atlantic Ocean has also been crucial, bringing with it an abundance of seafood that serves as the foundation for several regional specialties.

Must-Try Dishes

1. Fish Frito: Pescaíto Frito, a popular meal that is associated with Cadiz, is made out of various tiny local fish that are covered in flour and deep-fried until they are perfectly brown. Cuttlefish, sardines, and anchovies are often utilized to provide a delicious seafood experience with a crispy texture.

2. Tortillita de Camarones: A thin pancake flavored with chickpea flour and topped with small shrimp, or camarones, is a delicious dessert. The end product is a salty, crunchy treat that perfectly embodies the tastes of the coast of Cadiz.

3. Salmorejo: Although salmorejo is a cuisine that is typical of all of Andalusia, Cádiz adds its own special touch. This chilled tomato soup is thicker than gazpacho and is often served with jamón (cured ham) and hard-boiled eggs for a satisfying and cool meal.

4. Chocos a la Gaditana: There are many different methods to cook chocos, or cuttlefish, in Cadiz, but one particularly good meal is chocos a la Gaditana. To make a rich and tasty seafood stew, cuttlefish is usually cooked with potatoes, onions, garlic, and a mixture of fragrant spices.

5. Garbanzos with Espinacas: This traditional recipe calls for well-cooked spinach and chickpeas, which are often seasoned with cumin, paprika, and garlic. Simple as it may be, Espinacas with Garbanzos is a perfect example of the region's devotion to using only the best, freshest ingredients.

Popular Restaurants

1. El Faro: Cádiz's gastronomic landmark, El Faro, overlooks the Atlantic. This restaurant, which is well-known for its creative seafood dishes and authentic Andalusian cuisine, provides a panoramic view of the ocean and makes for an unforgettable dining experience.

2. Manteca Casa: Tucked away in the energetic La Viña neighborhood, Casa Manteca is a true gem. A local favorite, this rustic tapas bar serves up a range of traditional dishes paired with an eclectic assortment of regional wines and sherries.

3. Balandro: Known for its flawless service and fresh seafood, Balandro enjoys a prime location close to the Cádiz Cathedral. The menu features dishes that combine classic recipes with contemporary touches to produce a flavorful mashup.

4. La Candela: Known for its inventive use of regional products and cozy ambiance, La Candela is a hidden treasure in Cadiz. The chef's dedication to using seasonal ingredients guarantees a dynamic menu that changes to reflect the shifting tastes of the food world.

5. Juanito's Bar: Bar Juanito is a venerable business that was founded in 1935 and has endured over the years. Reputable for its adherence to traditional recipes, this family-run eatery serves up some of the best versions of Pescaíto Frito and other Cádiz staples.

In conclusion, Cadiz's food reflects the region's history, topography, and long-standing ties to the sea. Every meal narrates a tale of creativity and tradition, from the savory enticement of Chocos a la Gaditana to the crunchy joys of Pescaíto Frito. Discovering the well-known eateries, each with its own distinct character, offers a peek into the thriving food scene that makes Cádiz a must-visit location for foodies looking for a genuine Andalusian experience.

CHAPTER SEVEN: DAY TRIPS AND EXCURSIONS

Situated on Spain's southwest coast, the ancient city of Cadiz has a wealth of options for day trips and excursions. Visitors may fully experience the rich culture and stunning natural surroundings that this region has to offer, from immaculate beaches to enthralling historical places nearby.

Cadiz: A Synopsis
One of the oldest towns in Europe to have been inhabited continuously, Cadiz offers a unique combination of culture, history, and beautiful scenery. Understanding the city itself is crucial before exploring the many day trips and excursions.

Nearby Beaches
Cádiz, which was established by the Phoenicians in 1100 BC, has been influenced by several

civilizations, such as the Roman, Moor, and Visigoth. Its historical importance stems from its advantageous position as a port city, which has created a melting pot of numerous influences. The city's historic core is a tangle of winding streets, bustling squares, and old buildings that tell stories about its history.

Contemporary Cádiz
Cádiz has welcomed modernization while maintaining its traditional beauty. In addition to the city's well-preserved historical landmarks, visitors may enjoy a thriving culinary scene, bustling marketplaces, and modern attractions.

Day Journeys from Cadiz

1. Convenient beaches
Famous for its breathtaking beaches, Cadiz gives guests the opportunity to unwind by the Atlantic

Ocean's glistening waves. Here are a few noteworthy choices for day visits to the beach:

a. Victoria Beach
Playa de la Victoria is a vibrant urban beach with golden beaches that stretches along the coast within the city. It's the ideal location for beach activities, tanning, and dining at beachside eateries serving fresh seafood.

b. The Barrosa Beach
Playa de la Barrosa is a spotless beach with fine white sand and crystal-clear blue seas, only a short drive from Cádiz. It's a great place to spend a peaceful day by the sea, and there are many food choices along the promenade.

c. Baelo Claudia Archaeological Site and Bolonia Beach
The Bolonian Ocean is a great place to combine history with the ocean. In addition to its natural

beauty, Baelo Claudia, a well-preserved Roman archeological monument, is located on this beach. After seeing historic ruins, relax on the beach.

2. Historical Places in the Neighborhood

For those who like history, the area around Cadiz is full of interesting historical sites that make for interesting day trips:

a. La Frontera de Jerez

Jerez de la Frontera, an equestrian mecca and a short drive from Cádiz, is well-known for its sherry production. Wander through the quaint old town, visit Sherry Bodegas, and investigate the Royal Andalusian School of Equestrian Art.

a. Crossing the border

Vejer de la Frontera, a charming whitewashed hamlet with winding alleyways and a Moorish castle, is perched on a hill. The village is a refuge for people looking for true Andalusian charm and provides stunning views of the surrounding countryside.

c. Tarifa
Travel to Tarifa, the southernmost tip of continental Europe. This seaside town has a lively atmosphere, is a Moorish stronghold, and is a haven for lovers of water sports.

c. Old Town and the Cathedral in Cadiz
You may spend a day touring Cádiz's historic center without ever leaving the city. Two must-see sites are the Cádiz Cathedral, which has a golden dome, and the Torre Tavira, which has panoramic views. Explore the winding lanes to find hidden treasures such as Plaza de las Flores and Plaza de la Catedral.

Organizing Your Day Trip

Organizational logistics

Think about your transportation alternatives while organizing day excursions. Although guided excursions and public transit are also available, renting a car offers more freedom. Verify the attraction's opening times as well as any scheduled special events.

Considering the seasons

Cádiz has pleasant winters and hot, dry summers due to its Mediterranean climate. Typically, the beach season lasts from late spring to early fall. When organizing outdoor events and historical site tours, take the weather into account.

In summary

With its mix of ancient landmarks and sun-kissed beaches, Cadiz provides a wide choice of day tours and excursions. This area offers the ideal fusion of the past and present for anybody looking for a cultural experience, a beach lover, or a history enthusiast. To ensure that your Andalusian vacation is really memorable, spend some time exploring the neighboring beaches and learning about the rich history of Cádiz and its environs.

CHAPTER EIGHT: OUTDOOR ACTIVITIES

In addition to being rich in history and culture, Cádiz is a lovely city on Spain's southwest coast that provides a wealth of outdoor activities for people looking for fun and leisure. Cádiz offers a wide choice of activities to suit a variety of interests, making it a paradise for thrill-seekers and nature lovers alike. These activities include thrilling water sports and beautiful parks and gardens.

Parks and Gardens

Park Genovés
In the center of Cadiz, Parque Genovés is a verdant sanctuary that beckons both inhabitants and tourists to enjoy the splendor of the natural world. Well-kept lawns, colorful flowerbeds, and tall palm trees make the park a peaceful haven from the

hustle and bustle of the city. Strolling around the park's meandering walkways, admiring the wide variety of plant species, or just unwinding on one of the numerous seats are all options for visitors.

Apodaca Alameda
Alameda Apodaca is a rare combination of historical importance and natural beauty, nestled between the sea and the ancient city center. This large park is the perfect place for a romantic walk at sunset or a leisurely afternoon picnic since it provides stunning views of the Atlantic Ocean. The calm settings of the park are enhanced by the well-preserved statues and monuments that provide a hint of cultural richness.

Varela Gardens
One of Cadiz's hidden gems is Jardines de Varela, which is close to the well-known Caleta Beach. This little garden, with its elaborate fountains, rich flora, and quaint walks, radiates magic. The tranquil

sounds of trickling water and rustling foliage make this the ideal location for anybody looking for a quiet getaway.

Water Sports

At Playa de la Victoria, surfing
With its long coastline that is pounded by the Atlantic, Cadiz is a great place for lovers of water sports. For surfers of all skill levels, Playa de la Victoria is a paradise with its vast lengths of golden sand and steady waves. While more experienced surfers may push themselves with the more difficult breakers further out to sea, beginners can learn from local surf schools.

In Tarifa, kitesurfing
A quick trip to Tarifa, dubbed the windsurfing and kitesurfing capital of Europe, is a must for thrill-seekers. Kitesurfing is made possible by the powerful Levante and Poniente winds that blow

over the Strait of Gibraltar. All skill levels are catered for by the abundance of kiteboarding courses and rental facilities, so anybody may enjoy the exhilaration of soaring over the waves.

Canoeing in the Cádiz Bay
Kayaking the Bay of Cadiz is a unique opportunity to see the coastal splendor of the city. Canoe past the San Sebastián Castle, through the old city walls, and into undiscovered bays. For those seeking a guided experience, there are kayaking trips that provide information on the history and marine life of the region while enjoying physical exercise.

Snorkeling in the Aceite Islands
Cala del Aceite is a beautiful bay with pristine waters that are great for snorkeling. There is an abundance of marine life in this underwater environment, including vivid coral formations and colorful fish. Snorkelers may enjoy the peace of the

underwater world while exploring marine life at their own speed.

In summary

In summary, Cádiz is a location with several facets that skillfully combine breathtaking outdoor activities with unmatched natural beauty. Cádiz has a wide variety of activities for those who like the outdoors and adventure, whether they are more drawn to the calm atmosphere of parks and gardens or the adrenaline of water sports. The city's lively culture and rich history add to its allure, making it a must-visit for anybody looking for the ideal balance of adventure and leisure in the heart of Andalusia.

CHAPTER NINE: NIGHTLIFE

The busy nightlife of Cádiz, a picturesque seaside city in southwest Spain, draws both residents and visitors. After the sun goes down, the city comes alive with a variety of clubs, pubs, and entertainment venues that cater to night owls' varied interests. We will dive into the fascinating world of Cádiz's nightlife in this in-depth tour, taking in the city's distinctive pubs and clubs as well as the several entertainment venues that add to the vibrant after-dark scene.

Bars and Pubs

Famous for its scenic shoreline, Cadiz's taverns and pubs also have an air of charm. Several noteworthy places that contribute to the vibrant bar culture in the city are as follows:

1. El Faro de Cádiz: This famous pub is close to the central market and has beautiful sea views. It's the ideal place to have a drink and watch a beautiful sunset. El Faro is popular among both residents and tourists because of its delicious tapas and broad wine selection.

2. La Candela: Tucked away in Cádiz's ancient neighborhood, La Candela has a warm, welcoming atmosphere. This pub is well-known for its creative concoctions and handcrafted brews. Because the bartenders here are enthusiastic about mixology, customers looking for unusual and well-created cocktails are guaranteed a fantastic experience.

3. Taberna Casa Manteca: This place is a must-see for anybody wishing to become fully immersed in the culture of the area. Entired by bullfighting memorabilia, this historic pub gives a true Andalusian experience. Visitors may enjoy a selection of sherries, local cheese, and traditional cured ham here.

4. Freiduría Las Flores: Although it is primarily a seafood restaurant, as the evening wears on, Freiduría Las Flores develops into a bustling social center. This place is well-known for its fried fish, which is a specialty in the area, and customers often spill out into the streets, making for a lively environment.

5. Café Royalty: Experience the grace of the past at this historic location that blends contemporary conveniences with the allure of a bygone period. This chic pub that was once a café is ideal for those who want a little elegance in their evening. Live music events enhance this establishment's appeal.

Entertainment Venues

Outside of taverns and pubs, Cádiz has a wide range of entertaining options to suit different preferences. The city offers something for everyone, from theater productions to live music.

1. Gran Teatro Falla: Citing Cádiz's rich cultural legacy, Gran Teatro Falla is one of the city's architectural treasures. Ballets, theatrical performances, and concerts of classical music are just a few of the activities held in this ancient theater. Taking in a show here offers a cultural immersion into Cádiz's creative spirit.

2. Plaza de la Catedral: Especially on summer evenings, Plaza de la Catedral is the hub of the city. This open area, which is encircled by old buildings, is used for festivals and outdoor performances. With a lively environment beneath the stars, it's a popular meeting spot for both residents and visitors.

3. Sala Supersonic: For individuals who like live music, indie, rock, and alternative music genres are popular at Sala Supersonic. Local and international musicians perform in this little space, which electrifies the atmosphere and appeals to music lovers.

4. Cádiz Comedy Club: Everyone enjoys a good laugh, and the Cádiz Comedy Club makes sure that both residents and tourists get their fill of comedy. Comedians from both established and up-and-coming stages perform stand-up at this comedy club, making for a fun and lively evening.

5. La Quemá: The main attraction of La Quemá is flamenco, which has its roots in Andalusian culture. With passionate dancers, heartfelt singers, and accomplished guitarists enthralling the audience, this small flamenco arena provides a genuine experience. In the center of Cadiz, flamenco's intense emotional content comes to life.

In summary

To sum up, Cadiz's nightlife offers an intriguing fusion of the old and the new. Cádiz has a wide variety of possibilities for an unforgettable night out, whether your preference is for live concerts in historic locations, indulging in the local pub culture, or sipping drinks while taking in the sea view. In addition to its rich cultural legacy, Cádiz's friendly and inviting ambiance guarantees that its nightlife is really amazing. In the heart of Andalusia, the city comes to life when night sets, beckoning you to discover its hidden treasures and make lifelong memories.

CHAPTER TEN: SHOPPING

Shopping in Cadiz, Spain, is a lively and varied experience that combines distinctive mementos that encapsulate the spirit of this ancient city with typical local markets. Shopping options in Cádiz are many, ranging from quaint stores featuring artisan goods to lively markets where residents congregate to buy fresh vegetables. We'll explore the local markets in depth and learn about the distinctive mementos that contribute to the unforgettable and culturally rewarding shopping experience in Cádiz.

Local Markets

The Central Market of Abastos
The Mercado Central de Abastos in Cadiz is a bustling 19th-century marketplace that is a popular meeting area for both residents and tourists.

Situated near the center of the city, this market honors Andalusian cuisine. It provides a genuine window into Cádiz's everyday life with its lively atmosphere and rainbow of colors.

Seafood and fresh produce

As you meander through the aisles of the market, you'll come across a multitude of booths filled to the brim with fresh produce, fish, and fruits. For foodies looking for premium products, the market is a haven, offering everything from the catch of the day to local delicacies like salted fish and red shrimp.

Regional Tastes and Snacks

The Mercado Central de Abastos is a veritable gold mine of regional tastes and specialties in addition to fresh products. Cheese, cured ham, olive oil, and a range of spices invite guests to savor Andalusian cuisine. Samples are available from several vendors, so you may enjoy the region's richness.

Regionalh on the Plaza of the Flowers

The Mercado de la Plaza de las Flores is a little flower market in the center of Cadiz that offers a more personal purchasing experience. This market has a laid-back vibe, and it's flanked by charming cafés and old buildings.

Floral Extravaganza

The market focuses on flowers, plants, and gardening supplies, as the name would imply. Locals often go there to pick up ornamental plants or fresh flowers to put in their houses. A pleasant sensory experience is produced by the strong colors and scents.

Cafés and regional specialties

Next to the flower market are tiny restaurants and cafés that serve regional specialties. Suck down a croissant or have a cup of coffee and take in the gorgeous surroundings. Because of its position, the market is the ideal place to relax and take in the distinct character of the city.

Unique Souvenirs

Handmade ceramics from the La Viña neighborhood

The district of Barrio de la Viña is home to talented artists carrying on the centuries-old heritage of traditional pottery, which has made Cadiz famous worldwide. As you meander around the winding lanes, you'll come across galleries and stores displaying a beautiful collection of ceramics that have been hand-painted.

The influence of Talavera de la Reina

The old Spanish pottery town of Talavera de la Reina has had a major influence on Cádiz ceramics. Plates, tiles, and ornamental items are decorated with vivid colors, complex patterns, and representations of regional scenery. These exquisitely created ceramics are eternal mementos that encapsulate the spirit of Cádiz's creative past.

Calle Ancha Leather Products

One of Cádiz's major shopping avenues, Calle Ancha, is home to several leather businesses selling an extensive array of high-quality items. Handcrafted leather purses, wallets, and belts are just a few of the goods that these artists expertly make, expertly fusing traditional craftsmanship with contemporary design.

Spanish Tradition of Leathercraft

The items on Calle Ancha are a reflection of the rich history of Spanish leathercraft. These pieces are not only fashionable accessories but also long-lasting keepsakes of your trip to Cadiz because of the use of fine leather, meticulous attention to detail, and a dedication to quality.

Wine and Sherry

Cadiz is well known for producing the renowned Spanish wine, and it is one of the main towns in the Sherry Triangle. Buying a bottle of Sherry from a neighborhood bodega may be a unique way to carry a little piece of Cádiz home, even if it's not a typical souvenir.

Bodegas and Encounters with Tastings

Discover antique bodegas in Cádiz's streets, where you may taste and learn about the many types of sherry produced. A few bodegas provide guided tours that shed light on the history of the city's wine industry. A bottle of regionally made sherry is a unique and genuine present.

In summary

Shopping in Cadiz is a wonderful trip through its markets and shops, each providing a different viewpoint on the diversity of the city's culture. These marketplaces, which range from the bustling Mercado Central de Abastos to the quaint Mercado de la Plaza de las Flores, highlight the colorful lifestyle of Cadiz. In the meanwhile, a variety of distinctive mementos that encapsulate the essence of this ancient Spanish city may be found in the handmade pottery of Barrio de la Viña, the leather items of Calle Ancha, and the internationally recognized Sherry. Fresh local products, handcrafted goods, or a taste of Cádiz's culinary legacy can all be found in the city's varied retail district, which is guaranteed to make an impact

CHAPTER ELEVEN: PRACTICAL INFORMATION

Situated on Spain's southwest coast, the ancient city of Cadiz is a captivating fusion of culture, history, and breathtaking scenery. These crucial pointers will help you have an unforgettable and hassle-free vacation to Cadiz, whether you're planning a quick getaway or a longer stay.

1. Weather and Ideal Time to Go: Cadiz has a Mediterranean climate, meaning that summers are hot and dry and winters are moderate and damp. The ideal seasons to go are spring (April to June) and autumn (September to October), when the weather is nice and there are fewer tourists.

2. Money and Payment: The Euro (EUR) is the recognized currency. Hotels, restaurants, and bigger stores take most credit cards, but smaller businesses and street sellers may not, so bring cash.

3. Language: Cádiz's official language is Spanish. Even though most people who live and work in tourist destinations know English, it might still be beneficial to learn a few simple Spanish words to improve your interactions.

4. Transportation: Local trains and buses are part of Cádiz's effective public transportation network. There are also plenty of taxis available. Wear comfortable shoes if you want to explore the city on foot since many of the streets are cobblestone.

5. Local Food: Take advantage of the chance to savor the seafood delicacies of Cadiz. Taste the "tortillitas de camarones" (shrimp fritters) and "pescaíto frito" (fried fish). For a true taste of the area, pair your meals with wine or sherry.

6. Cultural Etiquette: Spanish people are renowned for their kind welcome. People are usually greeted with a handshake or two cheek kisses. It's customary to savor your food and take in the conversation while eating.

7. Siesta Tradition: Be aware that during siesta, many establishments shut for a few hours in the afternoon. Make appropriate plans for your activities and get into the local way of life.

8. Safety Advice: Although Cadiz is a relatively safe city, it's advisable to exercise caution. Be watchful about your possessions, particularly in busy places, and use caution while on public transit.

9. Clothes Code: When touring Cádiz, wear comfortable but presentable clothing. Make sure you wear modest clothing that covers your knees and shoulders if you want to attend places of worship.

10. Venture Beyond the Old Town: For a more authentic experience, don't be afraid to explore neighboring districts like La Viña and El Pópulo, even if the historic Old Town is a must-visit.

Emergency Contacts

1. Emergency Services:
Emergencies in Medicine:
112 Ambulance
Puerta del Mar Hospital: +34 956 005 000

Law enforcement: Emergencies: 112
Police in the area: +34 956 292 100

Fire Service:
Emergency: 112
Fire Department of Cadiz: +34 956 292 023.

2. Consulates: Get in touch with your consulate in Cádiz if you need help from your own nation. Here are a handful of the city's consulates:

Consulate of the United States: +34 915 872 200

Consulate of the United Kingdom: +34 913 342 194

Consulate of Canada: +34 915 236 097

3. Drugstores:

+34 956 257 083 for Farmacia San Felipe

+34 956 258 793 at Farmacia La Palma

4. Traveler Information

For general support and details:

- 902 102 365 for tourist information; - +34 956 241 001 for the tourist office in Cadiz.

5. Misplaced or stolen items:

Cádiz Police: +34 956 292 100; Lost and Found Emergency Number for Lost or Stolen Visa Credit Cards: 303-967-1096

6. Embassies in Madrid: Get in touch with your embassy in Madrid if you want help beyond what the consulates in Cádiz can provide.
Embassy of the United States: +34 915 872 200
Embassy of the United Kingdom: +34 917 146 300
Embassy of Canada: +34 915 236 082

In case of an emergency, don't forget to save these numbers on your phone and have a printed copy on hand. Have fun when visiting Cádiz!

CHAPTER TWELVE: CONCLUSION

Final Thoughts on Cádiz

Visitors from all over the globe are drawn to Cádiz, a medieval city tucked away on Spain's southwest coast, by its rich tapestry of culture, history, and natural beauty. As we come to the end of our tour of this fascinating place, it is important to consider all of the many facets that contribute to Cádiz's distinctive and unforgettable experience. The unique qualities of the city, from its historic foundation to its contemporary charm, create a lasting impression on those who are lucky enough to explore its cobblestone streets.

Historical Importance:

With more than three millennia of history, Cadiz is one of the oldest continuously inhabited towns in Western Europe. The sounds of its illustrious history vibrate through the air as we finish our trek through its winding lanes. Cádiz has been shaped by the Phoenicians, Romans, Moors, and other civilizations, leaving a historical mosaic that is shown at every step.

A major factor in the city's growth was its advantageous coastal position, which promoted a vibrant economy and cross-cultural interchange. The Cathedral of Cádiz, a magnificent example of Spanish Baroque architecture, and the famous Tavira Tower, which bears witness to the city's maritime heritage, are only two examples of the city's old origins.

Architectural Magnificence:
Cádiz's architectural environment is evidence of the city's skill in fusing the ancient with the modern. Cádiz is a visual feast for those who like a variety of architectural styles, from the tiny lanes of the Old Town with its whitewashed homes embellished

with wrought-iron balconies to the contemporary skyscrapers that punctuate the skyline.

An ancient city gate called Puertas de Tierra acts as a metaphorical border between Cádiz's old and modern neighborhoods. As our tour comes to an end, we can't help but be amazed by the contrast between the modern buildings that define the city's character and the historic defenses.

The Cultural Tapestry
Cadiz is a city of cultures, where customs, music, and artwork come together to form a rich mosaic of human expression. Cádiz's annual carnival, which is among the most renowned worldwide, is a vibrant celebration that perfectly captures the essence of the city. As we say goodbye to this festival, it leaves a lasting impression on our memories, demonstrating the city's capacity for happiness and celebration.

With its deep roots in Andalusian culture, flamenco has a particularly strong home in Cadiz. Our research is accompanied by the beautiful tunes and passionate rhythms that reverberate throughout the streets. As our trip draws to an end, Cádiz's rich cultural legacy becomes a treasured memento and a constant reminder of the city's dedication to conserving and honoring its history.

Gourmet Treats:
A visit to Cádiz wouldn't be complete without sampling its cuisine. The cuisine of the city is a lovely blend of sea and land, with fresh seafood holding a prominent position. Cádiz welcomes guests to go on a gastronomic adventure, from the busy Mercado Central, where sellers proudly show their catch of the day, to the charming tapas cafes nestled away in little lanes.

Pescaíto frito, or fried fish, is the region's signature dish and a superb example of Andalusian cuisine's simplicity and excellence. The aromas of Cádiz remain on our palates as we wrap off our gastronomic adventure, serving as a delectable reminder of the city's dedication to culinary excellence.

Natural Wonders:

Cadiz's urban charm is captivatingly set against a background of natural beauty. The immaculate beaches, including Playa de la Victoria, provide a peaceful haven where people may walk along the promenade or take in the sun. The Atlantic Ocean's rhythmic waves provide a calming lullaby as we wrap off our journey of these coastal beauties, serving as a constant reminder of nature's enduring effect on the city.

The botanical park Parque Genovés, with its lush vegetation and colorful blossoms, offers a welcome diversion from the city. As we say goodbye to this sanctuary, one aspect of our trip that stands out is how well nature and city life combine in Cadiz.

Communal Spirit:
The genuine spirit of Cadiz is found in its people's friendliness and kindness. There's a feeling of togetherness in the air as we wrap up our encounters with residents at quaint cafés and lively marketplaces. The warmth and friendliness of the Gaditanos add to the friendly environment of the city, giving tourists a feeling of inclusion.

The Plaza de las Flores, surrounded by bustling cafés and covered with vibrant flowers, perfectly captures the essence of Cádiz's sense of community. Looking back on our interactions with residents, it is clear that the city's spirit is built by sincere relationships between people as much as by its historical sites.

Last Words:

As we approach the end of our tour of Cádiz, it is evident that this city is more than just a place to visit; rather, it is a living example of how history, culture, and modernity have merged. Its historic streets, breathtaking buildings, vibrant cultural events, mouthwatering food, breathtaking scenery, and sense of community all combine to create an experience that is above and beyond the norm.

We will always remember Cádiz for its colorful streets, mouthwatering food, energetic music, and friendly locals as we say goodbye to this beautiful city. The end of our trip doesn't mean the end of the city's enduring charm; rather, it means that visitors still have time to experience the wonder of Cadiz.

Printed in Great Britain
by Amazon